Momma Said There Be Days Like This...

But Momma You Didn't Say That...

ALVINIA EPPES QUARLES

Copyright © 2016 by Alvinia Eppes Quarles

Momma Said There Be Days Like This... But Momma You Didn't Say That...
by Alvinia Eppes Quarles

Printed in the United States of America.

Edited by Xulon Press.

ISBN 9781498484947

All rights reserved solely by the author. The author guarantees all contents are original and do not infringe upon the legal rights of any other person or work. No part of this book may be reproduced in any form without the permission of the author. The views expressed in this book are not necessarily those of the publisher.

Unless otherwise indicated, Scripture quotations taken from the King James Version (KJV) – *public domain*.

www.xulonpress.com

TABLE OF CONTENTS

Dedication................................... vii
Introduction.................................. ix

Chapter 1: Momma............................11
Chapter 2: What Momma said about church 15
Chapter 3: What Momma said about marriage........21
Chapter 4: What Momma said about children 25
Chapter 5: What Momma said about health 27
Chapter 6: What Momma said about grief 31

About the Author................................35

DEDICATION

This book is dedicated to my mother, Dorothy M. Eppes. I consider her my greatest fan, and the strength that kept me going throughout my life. She and God have made me the woman that I have become. My mother went to be with the Lord in 2004, and the answers to a lot of questions that a daughter would ask her mother went with her.

INTRODUCTION

I am considered the older of five children; my parents had three boys and two girls. My mother was a strict disciplinarian in our home, so what my mother would say was the law in our home. She was an awesome wife and mother. She greatly respected my father, and ensured that everybody yielded to the fact that he was the head of our home.

Growing up, we were happy and healthy. Our home was small, but very clean. The way I was raised, I assumed all my friends had the same rules and disciplines that I did; yet as I grew up, I realized that it wasn't so. All the siblings had a unique relationship with our mother, as we could talk to her about anything; no topic was off-limits. My mom was also a very hard worker outside of the home. She worked as a supervisor at a dress factory, and she loved it; at least, that's what I thought. I never heard her complain about anything. Needless to say, every holiday the girls had very unique dresses, especially at Easter.

I knew my mother was a caring and thoughtful woman, but I didn't realize how much until I became a teenager. She was giving, and she opened up her home to anyone. I remember kids from the neighborhood that would stay in our home regularly. I also remember my mom telling me about a woman that ran from her husband, due to abuse, and found refuge in our home. I had friends that would come to her for advice about many things, for she would counsel them as if they were her own. My mom was very courageous in her advice.

In this book, you will find several topics of conversation between a mother and daughter. These topics will address a mother's attempts to prepare her daughter for life challenges. Some of the questions that I, as a daughter may have, did not surface until I became an adult. What inspired me to write this book was being in the company of young women that appeared to not have been prepared for what life would throw at them. They were under the impression that marriage would be perfect, it would be easy to have children, and that being a woman was going to be easy. This book allows me to voice the questions that I wished I knew to ask my mother before the challenges came. Some answers to the questions in life would have remained unanswered, if it wasn't for God. I pray this help others look to God for help with the challenges of this life.

Chapter 1

"MOMMA"

Growing up in a little town called Rice, Virginia was not difficult; the area in which we lived was surrounded by family. Our home was known as the white house on the hill. This wasn't because we were rich, but because we were the only white house on the road that sat on a hill. My grandmother lived only yards away; so close in fact that we could yell out of the kitchen window, and if her bedroom window was open, she could hear us. We lived in an area surrounded by trees, fruit and flowers. There were apple trees, pear trees, walnut trees, cherry trees, plumbs and persimmons. Also, strawberries and blackberries were everywhere; all the things that you take for granted as a child. The smell in the air was that of honeysuckles.

My mother had a garden filled with a variety of vegetables, which included greens of every kind, beans of every kind, tomatoes, cucumbers, potatoes, sweet potatoes, and the list goes on. She loved her garden and took pride in it, forbidding anyone access to her garden without her permission. Everything around me was green and flourishing. We had lots of room to run and play in safety: no streets; only roads in which the majority of people that traveled it were family.

I grew up with six siblings, so it was never a dull or boring moment. Society would have called my older brother, my half-brother, but Mom taught us that there was no such thing as a half-brother. She taught us that we were all brothers and sisters, and will be treated as such. However, I was the oldest girl, and the expectations of being the oldest were taken very seriously.

Momma was the disciplinarian in the family, so she could be tough but she was fair. When we were left alone with our dad and we would get in trouble, Dad would say, "Wait until your mom comes". She did not tolerate lying or fighting with your siblings; supporting and loving each other was the key. Mom taught us to love your family and to always be there for each other. She taught that we should never fight each other and always seek to reconcile our differences immediately. I listened and watched how family members would treat her, for she had such grace and would never retaliate. There were times that I was not that graceful. My cousin pushed me and when I hit him, I dislocated my finger. I couldn't tell my mother about the pain that I was experiencing, because that would mean that I disobeyed her and hit my cousin. So, in other words, my finger is still crooked to this day.

I grew up in an era in which everyone worked, including the kids. Every sibling had chores to do, including the smallest sibling. Remember when it was considered "hog killing season"? The men were responsible for killing the hog and prepping it, while the women were waiting in the house to do everything else. I recall to mind one particular season in which my mom, grandmother and aunts were in the kitchen, waiting for the big aluminum tin to come in the house with all the hog innards in it. It was nasty looking and smelled bad, but these were our provisions for the year, and YOU DARE NOT COMPLAIN. I watched as my mom tore the intestines and cut them; chitterlings we call it. My assignment was to pour water over my mother's hands as she cleaned chitterlings; YOU DARE NOT COMPLAIN. Other siblings were to pour the water out, wipe the floor and served as runners between outside help and inside help. She taught us that we have to work for what we get; we would appreciate it.

My mother and father provided for us the best they knew how, making sure we had all the necessities of life. My mother taught us to always be thankful for what you have, because there was always someone worse off than you. Her words came true when I went to my friend's house and could see outside through the walls of her home. That was quite an eye-opener, and it gave me great appreciation for what I had. My mother always looked for someone in the neighborhood to help and would say, "There is always someone worse off then you." My mother warned us to never speak of what we gave to others. Even when you saw someone wearing your clothes or shoes, it would be detrimental to you to say anything.

My mom was active in her church and made sure that we attended church regularly. She was a member of a singing group called the Spiritual Sisters, in which her mom was the leader. I would travel with them often and people loved them. They had beautiful voices and worked well together. In my childlike mind, they were famous, and I was proud to be affiliated with them. However, I never thought I would have the courage to stand before people and sing anything. My mother would always tell me I had a beautiful voice and, at the time, I found that hard to believe.

My mom was an awesome cook, and her kitchen was a great place to talk to her and acquire her words of wisdom. Our conversations contained subjects of boys, school and general questions about being a respectable woman. She told me to be nice and treat others well. She taught me to give and to not expect anything in return. She taught me to not tell everyone everything, to be discreet. She also said, "Never believe what you hear and believe little of what you see".

Chapter 2

"CHURCH"

What Momma said about Church…

Church was a place that you received the Word of God, which is to bring life to the hearer. The Word of God says, "Train up a child in the way he should go: and when he is old, he will not depart from it" (Prov. 22:6). As a child, church was a place that you go on Sunday morning, because it was Sunday. I didn't completely understand the whole purpose for going to church. I remember hearing about a God that I didn't understand and a sacrifice of a son, Jesus, which I couldn't comprehend. However, out of obedience, I did what I was told with no complaints.

My mother loved to play the piano and would say to me, "You need to play the piano because you have piano fingers." Like many young women, I would complain and say, "I don't want to play." Momma would say, "You are going to wish you have played the piano one day"; Momma was right about that. Because now, knowing how to play the piano would be an asset to our church.

My mom would say to me, "Pick something in the church to do, because you will do something." My mom believed in working for the Lord. As a child, I saw it as working for my grandmother, since she appeared to be the one in charge. I chose to usher while Momma chose the choir for me, so I did both. The best thing about them both is that my cousins were doing the same thing that I did.

We had very strict Momma rules in church: "No talking in church, no chewing gum and no playing," Momma said. However, my cousins and I always found a way to communicate, even though for some reason she always knew and we always got in trouble. It appeared as though everyone in the church were in our conversation so if you did anything, Momma would always find out.

One of the benefits of my mom working in a dress factory was that we had beautiful dresses to wear to church. Attending church was a must in my home; Momma said, "I don't care where you go on Saturday night, or what time you come in, but you will be in church on Sunday morning." Momma was serious, as you dare not say you are tired. Growing up in our church, there was no such thing as "children's church". Children's church was sitting next to a relative and keeping your ears open and your mouth shut. Momma would quiz you when you returned home to make sure that you were not playing nor talking, but listening to the pastor.

The church in which I attended as a child was ninety percent family. Everyone in the church knew each other. loved each other and had a mutual respect for each other. I remember when the pastor was at my grandmother's house for dinner one Sunday. The children could not come into

"Church"

house while the pastor was there. We were fed and sent outside to play. Momma taught us to respect the pastor with no exceptions.

What Momma didn't say about Church.....

As an adult, I left the church because I didn't see why it was important. Growing the church meant family and God. As a young lady, I believed the people who sang the church songs lived them. I believed that they sang to a God that they served and worshiped. I have learned that the same people that were singing godly songs were doing ungodly things. I believe that if Momma would have told me, I wouldn't have been so shocked and disappointed. I visited a church, and we were told to hold hands in a circle of prayer. I held hands with the pastor of that church. The thing that he did with his hand was inappropriate for a man of God. I didn't know what his relationship was with God, but I understood what type of relationship he wanted with me.

One day, my friend and I went to a concert in which it had many gospel greats of my time, such as Gospel Keynotes, Jackson Southerners', Mighty Clouds of Joy, to name a few. I was extremely excited about seeing them. I had such respect for these men, because they were singing for God. Upon returning home that night, we received a phone call from a member of one of those groups. The man on the other end of the line was flirting with me, and the conversation was not right. "Momma, you didn't say to watch out for pedophiles in the church," I thought. Church is supposed to be a place in which you got direction from God from the men and women of God. It, now, has come to a point in our church world in which the youth pastor has to have a background check. The pastor has to counsel with the door open. Keeping the door open is not so much to protect the person from the pastor, but to protect the pastor from the member. It is not advisable to let your child be alone with members of the clergy anymore. Sleepovers are not advised anymore. "It's sad, Momma," I think. The oppressor is in the church.

I have learned that the leaders in the church that preach the gospel do not live according to the gospel. There are pastors that are robbing the church. I have heard that unless the preacher gets paid, he will not speak the gospel. It appears that it is all about the pastors and what they can get out of the church members. It seems like some are selling the Gospel of Jesus Christ instead of preaching the gospel.

"Momma, I found the answer...."

The Word of God said in 1 Peter 5:8, "Be sober, be vigilant; because your adversary the devil, as a roaring lion, walketh about, seeking whom he may devour." I have learned that there is an enemy that is assigned to each one of us, and his objective is to destroy our walk with God. He is not selective on whom he will damage. The enemy has disguised himself as a friend, a teacher and/or a confidant. In 2 Corinthians 11:14, it reads, "And no wonder, even Satan disguises himself as an angel of light." He is set to destroy your self-esteem and keep you in total withdrawal from God and man.

Momma, I have learned that the Word of God is true. In 1 Timothy 4:1, it reads, "The Spirit says clearly that in later times some believers will desert the Christian faith.

They will follow spirits that deceive, and they will believe the teachings of demons." I know regardless of what others do for Christ, I will be held accountable for what I do. I must stand firm, do my best and let the Lord handle the rest. According to 1 Corinthians 15:58, "[58] Therefore, my beloved brethren, be ye stedfast, unmoveable, always abounding in the work of the Lord, forasmuch as ye know that your labour is not in vain in the Lord."

Chapter 3

"MARRIAGE"

What Momma said about marriage….

"One day, when you grow up and get married, then you will understand," Momma said. My mother was married to a wonderful man. He was a hard worker and cared deeply for his wife and family. I loved to watch my mom and dad interact with each other. I watched my mom take care of him, her children and her home. She respected my dad and considered him in any decisions that were made for the family; it appeared that they had a mutual respect for each other. At dinnertime, we were all assembled at the table; the boys on the left and the girls on the right. We all had assigned seating, and it never changed. We all sat and waited with our hands in our laps until our dad came to the table. Once Dad arrived, Mom would pray, and then we would eat. After dinner, my sister and I would clean the kitchen. My dad would commence to watch the six o'clock news in their bedroom; Mom made sure that we were quiet and didn't disturb my dad. We didn't mind or complain, as it was normal. I was also told by my mom that she and Dad have an arrangement. She would take care of the inside of the house, while he would take care of the outside. I thought this is what marriage is all about: respect, support and communication.

One day, Mom and Dad was arguing, but the argument didn't make sense to me. As a child, it felt horrible. How can this be the way a husband and wife treat each other? I watched as they fought each other, as though they were enemies, and the mirror on the dresser shattered. I remember running to my grandmother's house for help. Afterwards, I remember my mom telling me, "Don't trust no man completely." That's when I made my decision that I would never get married.

However, in August 1980, I married and moved away from home. I thought that my marriage would be different, and I decided we would not fight or argue. When I moved in with my husband, it was awesome. All I knew as a wife is what I learned from watching my mom, but he was so different.

What Momma didn't say about marriage....

Momma, I didn't know husbands could be so mean. I have learned so much being married, and being around and listening to other married women. My God, I wish I could have asked my mom: What do you do if your husband commits adultery? What do I do if he disrespects me? What do I do if he tries to control me? What if he hits me and my children? These subjects never came up. That husband that you showed me, that could be, is now someone to be feared.

I have been around women that have been left bruised and battered. I have been around women that not only had an insurance plan and medical plan, but also an escape plan; they found themselves hiding and running for their lives. They trusted their husbands, but the men violated that trust. I remember the reconciliation and the forgiveness that you showed me. However, the love and respect that you showed my father is nowhere to be found in their homes. Home is not a refuge, but a prison. I have heard the phrase "walking on eggshells" when around their spouses and heard husbands openly confess that they have a mistress; that the mistress has even borne him a child. It is very degrading for a woman to endure this. However, where will these women form the strength to go? I have been around wives where the husbands are verbally abusive. I never saw my mom and dad talk to each other in a degrading manner. Some families have children that are used as weapons to keep the wives in line. Mom never told me that there were some fathers that were having sexual relations with their daughters. Oh my God, Momma, if you would have shared this, I don't think I would have ever gotten married. The wife sits in shame and pain, wanting to tell but won't for the fear of reprisal. She can't find a reason to stay, but doesn't know how to leave.

"Momma, I found the answer...."

Momma, God does not approve of this behavior. I found what God said in Ephesians 5:25, 28: "Husbands, love your wives, even as Christ also loved the church, and gave himself for it;...So ought men to love their wives as their own bodies. He that loveth his wife loveth himself." I believe that men who do these things to women have deep-rooted issues within themselves that have not been dealt with at all.

In God's Word, He gave a charge to the family. In Colossians 3:18-21, it reads:

> [18] Wives, submit yourselves unto your own husbands, as it is fit in the Lord. [19] Husbands, love *your* wives, and be not bitter against them. [20] Children, obey *your* parents in all things: for this is well pleasing unto the Lord.[21] Fathers, provoke not your children *to anger*, lest they be discouraged.

God has set a standard for us to live, so He will be pleased with us. I have a saved husband who trust and believes God. I have also learned that above all the good men that we have in the world, a saved husband is the best husband. I am so blessed that he has given his life to the Lord; this makes it easy to have a peaceful marriage. Once your husband totally gives his life to the Lord, he will do everything in his power to remain pleasing to him. I have learned to pray continually for my husband; even if he is not saved yet, keep praying. For the abused wife, it is not your fault. God loves you; He knows and He cares.

Chapter 4

"CHILDREN"

What Momma said about children…

"When you have your own children, I hope they act just like you. When you have your own children, then you will understand what it feels like as a mother." Being the oldest in a house of five was challenging, for the oldest child was always responsible for the younger ones. I also have another brother, which society calls him my half-brother, but he is our whole brother. There is nothing half about him. My mother loved him, like she loved the rest of us. She used to tell me how she wanted to raise him in the home with the rest of us. Mom taught that being a mother includes your children by blood and your children by choice.

During school days, I had to make sure that we ate breakfast and the kitchen was cleaned before we left. Mom fixed oatmeal in the mornings, but as a child, I didn't like the thick oatmeal. So I would add more water when she left, so as far as she knew we enjoyed her oatmeal.

My mother was the disciplinarian in the family; whatever she said went. My dad respected that about her. He would say, when we got into trouble, "Wait until your mom gets home." She didn't believe in disrespecting adults and was taught that you obey adults. She taught that you do not fight your family, but were to always help them and be there for them.

Momma was very open in communicating with us. We could tell her anything, including sex. She said there was nothing that a child should not be able to talk to her mother about.

What Momma didn't say about children....

Momma, I didn't know that I wouldn't be safe in my uncle's house. Why is my uncle touching me this way? I don't like the hugs. What about children who respect the adults in school, like you said, but they hurt them? They respected the ministers in the church, but they hurt them. What do I say them, Momma? It's not all like you said. Children are committing suicide because of the shame that they experienced in their homes, schools and churches.

"Momma, I found the answer...."

Momma, God cares about this; He is not pleased with this behavior. I read in Mark 9:42, where it says, "And whosoever shall offend one of these little ones that believe in me, it is better for him that a millstone were hanged about his neck, and he were cast into the sea." We now tell our children to tell someone immediately after wrongdoing. Don't believe the lie that the offender tells them; we must tell them that the lie is the offenders' weapon of choice.

Chapter 5

"HEALTH"

What Momma said about health...
I remember every fall, my momma would line all of us in a row to give us medicine to keep all the illnesses away. She had one spoon and five mouths. We had to take something called black draw, which I think is how you spell it. It was totally nasty. We had to take vitamins called super de pearls; they looked like liquid-filled, brown marbles. I bit into a vitamin one day, but I won't do that again. She also gave us other things; needless to say, we didn't get sick. It was rare that any of us were sick. My momma taught us about being healthy and eating right. She taught us to take care of our bodies. She was an awesome cook and cooked everything from scratch, as well as had her own garden and livestock. Whatever we ate was from Mom's garden, on a tree or in a pasture.

Play time was outside, for video games and excessive TV watching was not allowed. We were scheduled regular medical exams and were taught that we should never ignore any pain and abnormality in our health. I remember as a child that we would hardly ever catch a cold. She would line us up and give us vitamins, and many other home remedies, to ward off any winter illnesses or diseases; everything taste bad.

I remember when Momma was diagnosed with cancer. Where did that come from? You handled that with such grace and strength, Momma. It was scary for me, but you would always say, "I'm gonna be alright." However, Mom, how do you catch cancer? How do I keep this from happening?

What Momma didn't say about health....

Momma, I have a lump in my breast; where did it come from? I ate the right things and exercise regularly. I don't believe I ate anything that would have caused this. Momma, you didn't prepare me for this. This thing is eating away at my body, and I can't do anything about it. I went in for a normal checkup, but the diagnosis was "There is something suspicious in your breast." Momma, you are not here. I can't ask you what to do. Biopsies? Chemo? Radiology? Who can understand? Now I find myself surrounded by doctors, surgeons and nurses. I need to talk to you and ask you what to do. Momma, I have to have chemotherapy and radiation. Momma, now what? Momma, I feel alone. Momma, what if.... Momma, who can relate to my fears? Your voice would be so helpful.

"Momma, I found the answer..."

Momma, I serve God. I'm saved and filled with His Holy Spirit. I will either believe in this God or not. The

"Health"

Bible says, in Hebrews 11:6, "...He that cometh to God must believe that he is, and the he is a rewarder of them that diligently seek him." I'm talking to God to give me direction. I ask Him to send the doctors in my life that can help me through this. I don't know who to choose, so I need God to do it for me. I still believe in miracles. Isaiah 53:6 says, "...with his stripes we are healed." I will remain calm, knowing that God is in control. Momma, I had the surgery, and the surgeon was awesome. I went through the chemotherapy. I expected it to be really bad; however, God bought me through. I kept going. I kept working. I kept living. I kept trusting. My family is so supportive. The cancer is gone. Momma, the doctors call me a cancer survivor, but I have my life back, and I am victorious.

Chapter 6

"GRIEF"

What Momma said about loss of loved ones.

My Bigma died (my grandmother). Oh my God; we had table talks. She answered my questions about God. She explained how the Holy Spirit feels. She talked to me about being a respected young lady: to be modest; don't be loud; be discreet. I felt life as I knew it was gone. Momma handled the loss of her mother with such grace. I cried; she hugged. I cried; she comforted. She comforted us and made us feel that everything would be alright. We were told to remember the good times and that she lives in our hearts. Momma moved forward and insisted that we did, too. I didn't understand where her strength came from. Momma, I had such a difficult time going to Bigma's house. Things aren't the same; the warmth was not there anymore. The house don't smell like her. How do I handle moving forward without her? Oh my God, my aunt. Not again, my uncle. Momma was so comforting and so loving. I made it through because you helped me.

What Momma didn't say about grief......

No, this can't be happening, Momma. Will it be alright now? Wait, you didn't tell me that I would have to grieve you. We didn't talk about this; I'm not ready. I can't do this without you. I have children. Where is my counsel coming from? Now who will I tell my secrets to? Where will my words of encouragement come from? Who will tell me it will be alright? I could count on your love. I could count on your honesty. I could count on your support. I don't want this. You are the only true love that I know. No matter my victories or failures, you are always there to cheer me on.

Ten years later, no Daddy; I don't like this. You didn't tell me I'd have to mourn for you and Daddy. I am Daddy's little girl and I need my daddy. I will never here "Hey baby" again. What a shock; you went too soon. This wasn't suppose to happen. How did such a small issue take you away from us? I never gave much thought to being in this world without you both. I don't know to live in this world without you both; I never had to. That was a lesson you never taught me. The house is so empty. The sound is not in the house anymore. The warmth is not there anymore. When I walked through the home, I remember going in your room. You on the left and Dad on the right. I remember sitting on the bed not to move around too much, because Dad didn't like it. The scanner is still on the night table; this is the first time I have been in our home and I don't hear the scanner. Mom, what am I gonna do? I feel like I am alone in the world for the very first time.

"Grief"

"Mom, I found the answer..."

Momma, I thought you would like to know I found an answer. I found comfort in my relationship with Christ. In Matthew 5:4, it says, "Blessed are they that mourn, they will be comforted." Jesus has wiped my tears away every time. I miss you, but He has been with me through it all. Through every tear, I find a reason to rejoice; not because you are not here, but because you are with Christ. One day, we will be together again.

ABOUT THE AUTHOR

Who is Alvinia Quarles? I have been married to a retired warrant officer for thirty-five years. I have traveled all other the world with my husband, via military assignment. I have had many challenges as a wife, especially a military wife. I have had to pack up and readjust my life over a twenty-five year period. I am a mother of three sons and two grandsons.

Currently, I live in Alaska and am now a pastor's wife. I never thought that would be on my resume of life. Now that's a challenge; having to share your husband with so many people. I am an evangelist missionary and am considered the Church Mother in our church. This allows me to counsel and train many women of all ages and stages of life.

In 2011, I was diagnosed with breast cancer. God has delivered me, and I am cancer-free. Through this experience, I have learned that God is real, and the love of those around me are genuine and real as well. Many women have crossed my path that I have been able to encourage. I learned during this time that true love does exist among us, and that it an action word.

In 2014, I lost five family members; one of the family members was my father, who passed in February, and my first cousin (who I considered as my sister) in March. Needless to say, I became acquainted with grief.

I have learned over the years to answer as many questions as I can based on my life experiences. I believe that whatever I can do to help young women to succeed is my imprint on life.

www.ingramcontent.com/pod-product-compliance
Ingram Content Group UK Ltd.
Pitfield, Milton Keynes, MK11 3LW, UK
UKHW022211230426
12048UKWH00016BA/780